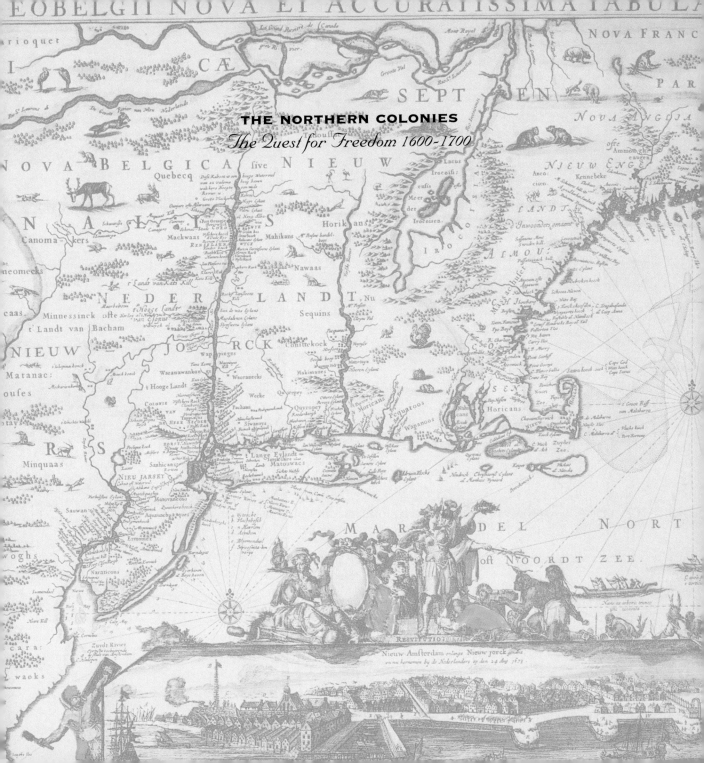

THE NORTHERN COLONIES

The Quest for Freedom 1600-1700

TITLE LIST

THE NORTHERN COLONIES:
The Quest for Freedom 1600-1700

BY
SHEILA NELSON

MASON CREST PUBLISHERS
PHILADELPHIA

Mason Crest Publishers Inc.
370 Reed Road
Broomall, Pennsylvania 19008
(866) MCP-BOOK (toll free)

First printing
1 2 3 4 5 6 7 8 9 10

Library of Congress Cataloging-in-Publication Data

Nelson, Sheila.
  The northern colonies : the quest for freedom (1600–1700) / by Sheila Nelson.
      p. cm. — (How America became America)
  Audience: Grades 9–12.
  ISBN 1-59084-901-9   ISBN 1-59084-900-0 (series)
  1. New England—History—Colonial period, ca. 1600–1775—Juvenile literature. 2. Middle Atlantic States—History—Colonial period, ca. 1600–1775—Juvenile literature. 3. Freedom of religion—New England—History—17th century—Juvenile literature. 4. Freedom of religion—Middle Atlantic States—History—17th century—Juvenile literature. I. Title. II. Series.
  F7.N45 2005
  974'.02—dc22
                              2004016629

Design by M.K. Bassett-Harvey.
Produced by Harding House Publishing Service, Inc.
Cover design by Dianne Hodack.
Printed in the Hashemite Kingdom of Jordan.

CONTENTS

CONTENTS

THE NORTHERN COLONIES

INTRODUCTION

by Dr. Jack Rakove

Today's America is not the same geographical shape as the first American colonies—and the concept of America has evolved as well over the years.

When the thirteen original states declared their independence from Great Britain, most Americans still lived within one or two hours modern driving time from the Atlantic coast. In other words, the Continental Congress that approved the Declaration of Independence on July 4, 1776, was continental in name only. Yet American leaders like George Washington, Benjamin Franklin, and Thomas Jefferson also believed that the new nation did have a continental destiny. They expected it to stretch at least as far west as the Mississippi River, and they imagined that it could extend even further. The framers of the Federal Constitution of 1787 provided that western territories would join the Union on equal terms with the original states. In 1803, President Jefferson brought that continental vision closer to reality by purchasing the vast Louisiana Territory from France. In the 1840s, negotiations with Britain and a war with Mexico brought the United States to the Pacific Ocean.

This expansion created great opportunities, but it also brought serious costs. As Americans surged westward, they created a new economy of family farms and large plantations. But between the Ohio River and the Gulf of Mexico, expansion also brought the continued growth of plantation slavery for millions of African Americans. Political struggle over the extension of slavery west of the Mississippi was one of the major causes of the Civil War that killed hundreds of thousands of Americans in the 1860s but ended with the destruction of slavery. Creating opportunities for American farmers also meant displacing Native Americans from the lands their ancestors had occupied for centuries. The opening of the west encouraged massive immigration not only from Europe but also from Asia, as Chinese workers came to labor in the California Gold Rush and the building of the railroads.

By the end of the nineteenth century, Americans knew that their great age of territorial expansion was over. But immigration and the growth of modern industrial cities continued to change the American landscape. Now Americans moved back and forth across the continent in search of economic opportunities. African Americans left the South in massive numbers and settled in dense concentrations in the cities of the North. The United States remained a magnet for immigration, but new immigrants came increasingly from Mexico, Central America, and Asia.

Ever since the seventeenth century, expansion and migration across this vast landscape have shaped American history. These books are designed to explain how this process has worked. They tell the story of how modern America became the nation it is today.

One
THE SEPARATISTS

The men marched silently through the cold early spring morning. Up ahead, they could see the ship they had hired to take them secretly out of England to the Netherlands, where people could freely worship as they saw fit. As they approached the shore, they saw a smaller boat beyond the ship, a little way along a creek. A few of the men smiled slightly. That would be their wives and children, along with all the baggage.

Someone waved from the ship, and several sailors began lowering a landing craft into the water. When the little boat reached them, the men climbed aboard, and the sailors rowed back across the bay to the Dutch ship. As they neared the ship, the men could see that the women's boat appeared to have run aground on a low-tide sandbar.

The men pulled themselves up the side of the ship on a rope ladder, and the landing craft prepared to make a trip out to pick up the women and children. The captain stood by the railing as the men climbed onto the deck, staring toward the creek where the women's boat lay stranded. Abruptly, he turned and shouted in Dutch to the sailors around him, then called down to those in the boat below. The sailors grabbed the ropes tossed down to them, secured the boat, and then scrambled up the rope ladder to the deck.

The Englishmen looked at each other in confusion. "What is happening?" one asked the captain. "What about our families?"

*To be taken into **custody** means to be placed under the control of someone else.*

"I will not let my ship fall into the hands of the English," the captain answered, gesturing toward shore.

The men turned to look where the captain pointed. A large group of men on horseback and on foot had just crested a little hill. The thin morning sunlight flashed on weapons. Someone must have discovered the group was trying to leave England illegally. They had been stopped before.

Pilgrims on the Mayflower

The sailors had hoisted the landing craft onto the deck, and the ship was beginning to turn its prow toward open water.

"What about our families?" one of the Englishmen cried again.

The captain did not answer him this time.

The men watched with horror as the armed men reached the boat in the creek. The wind carried the faint sound of crying children out to the Dutch ship. Several of the men fell to their knees on deck and sobbed. Others cried out prayers. Helplessly, they looked on as the armed men took their families into *custody*. The men had escaped, but without their wives, their children, or anything more than the clothes they wore.

In the spring of 1608, this group of English Separatists from Scrooby, in Nottinghamshire, fled on a Dutch ship from the mouth of the Humber River. Their wives and children, captured by English officials before they could board the ship, found passage later in the year to join their husbands in the Netherlands. The constables who had arrested the women had not known what to do with them. They released the group shortly after taking them into custody.

Replica of a sailing ship

During the fifty years before this, the idea of Puritanism had developed in England in reaction to Anglicanism. The Puritans believed England was right to leave the Roman Catholic Church and set up their own Anglican Church, but they thought the reforms had not gone far enough. They believed the church needed to be purified further by doing away with elaborate **rituals** and the church **hierarchy** of bishops and archbishops, and by following an exact interpretation of the Bible. Many Puritans thought the church could be reformed from within, but some believed reform was impossible. These Separatists removed themselves from the church altogether and met instead in their homes.

In England at this time, the law required people to attend Anglican Church services every week. Separatists were fined and sometimes thrown in jail for refusing to go to church. One group of Separatists began meeting in the home of William Brewster at Scrooby. After a decade of ***persecution*** for their beliefs, however, they longed to leave England and move to a place where they could worship freely. Unfortunately, English law also required them to get the king's permission before ***emigrating***. They knew King James would never let them leave just because they disagreed with the English laws on religion. They would have to sneak out of England illegally.

King James I believed strongly in the divine right of kings (the idea that the king is appointed by God and answers to him alone). Under this theory, any attempt to remove a king from power would be against the will of God. From his position just under God, James ruled the English church, as

Rituals *are formal ceremonies.*

*A **hierarchy** is a chain of command.*

Persecution *is discrimination, harassment, and treatment that can cause suffering and injury based on a belief, ethnicity, or race.*

Emigrating *means leaving your homeland to live somewhere else.*

The Houses of Parliment

King James

Subjects *are people who are ruled by a king or queen.*

well as England. After Henry VIII created the Church of England in the 1530s, English rulers held the title "Supreme Head of the Church of England."

The Puritans, and especially the Separatists, disagreed fervently with the divine right of kings. They believed that what God thought was more important than what the king thought. Parliament—the English government—sided more often with the Puritans than with the king. After all, James's view on the divine right of kings meant he did not have to listen to Parliament or take their advice. Meanwhile, King James worked hard to discourage Separatist churches. He was head of the Church of England, which he felt was only fitting in his God-appointed position, and he preferred his **subjects** to follow his lead on religion as well as on other matters.

The widening gap between James's views and those of Parliament created a difficult relationship. James spent money extravagantly and gave titles of nobility to those who supported him, which many saw as bribery. Parliament found James a frustrating and annoying king.

After James died and his son Charles came to the throne in 1625, the relationship between king and Parliament deteriorated even further. Charles believed his father's ideas about the divine rights of kings, and he kept up his father's excessive spending

Henry the VIII

habits as well. On top of this, however, Charles began to establish close ties with Catholic monarchs across Europe. Parliament worried this might mean Charles wanted to bring Catholicism back to England; Protestant Parliament could not stand that idea.

When Parliament objected to Charles's policies, Charles disbanded them. For eleven years, Charles ruled without Parliament. Without the support of Parliament, however, Charles had to

Charles I of England

Oliver Cromwell

raise his own money. Finally, he was forced to ask for their help again. Charles's need for money put him at the mercy of Parliament, and he reluctantly had to agree to fire his **ministers** Parliament did not like. Finally, King Charles I had had enough. He rebelled against the limitations Parliament had imposed on him and raised an army of his own to subdue them. Instead of taking back control, though, Charles was captured, and in 1649, he was beheaded. For the next eleven years, Parliament, under the control of the Puritan Oliver Cromwell, ruled England.

Unlike many of these later Puritans, who wanted to shape the government to their own ideals, the Separatists who fled to the Netherlands in 1608 wanted only the freedom to worship God in their own way. They found this freedom in the Netherlands, one of

Ministers are high-ranking government advisers.

New World or Old?

People often speak of the Americas as the "New World," while they refer to Europe as the "Old World." These terms make sense if you're thinking from a European point of view—but things look different from the perspective of people whose ancestors have lived in the Americas for thousands of years. If you belong to one of the many American Indian tribes, you'll probably think North and South America are the "old" world—and the Europeans, as relative newcomers on the scene, came from a "new" land across the sea. It's all a question of point of view.

*A **patent** is an exclusive privilege to use something for a specified period of time.*

the most tolerant countries in Europe when it came to religion, but they were still not happy. Most of the Separatists were farmers, used to living in small rural English towns. In the Netherlands, they lived in the city and worked as laborers. Everyone around them spoke Dutch, and the Separatists worried their children would grow up knowing nothing about their own English culture.

After ten years in the Netherlands, the Separatists wanted to move again. They wanted a place of their own, where they could live the way they wanted and worship the way they wanted. Some of the men traveled to England and talked to the Virginia Company about settling in the "New World." The Virginia Company, which had planted the Jamestown colony several years earlier, granted the Separatists a **patent** to settle on their land, and the Separatists prepared to make the long journey across the ocean.

America had only just begun to be settled by Europeans in 1620. The first (unsuccessful) colony had been planted less than thirty-five years before, and Jamestown had been settled in 1607. The white population of North America consisted of only a few hundred people, mostly in tiny settlements clustered around Jamestown. Meanwhile, Native American tribes lived in scattered bands across the North American continent. Most American Indians at this time had never encountered white men, although diseases carried across the Atlantic by European explorers over the past 128 years had already taken their toll on Native populations.

Very early in the seventeenth century, Indians in the rocky hills of New England had encountered some white explorers along their coast. In 1605,

Map of the Netherlands

An Invisible Killer

You may think that guns and swords were responsible for the European conquest of the Americas—but really an invisible killer wiped out far more Native people than did the Europeans' superior weapons. In the centuries after Columbus landed in the New World in 1492, more native North Americans died each year from infectious diseases brought by the European settlers than were born. Germs were the Indians' worst enemy.

Many types of diseases were brought into the Americas; the main ones were smallpox, measles, influenza, and typhus, as well as whooping cough, the mumps, and diphtheria. When a person is exposed to the germs that cause these illnesses, he will usually become ill. If he does not die, however, his body will have created antibodies to protect him from becoming infected again by the same germs. In other words, he will have immunity to that particular germ.

Many types of infectious diseases are carried by animals and passed along to humans. Europeans lived close to various types of domestic animals, and so they had plenty of opportunities to come in contact with many types of infectious disease and develop immunities. Each generation had also developed genetic material that made people more resistant to disease. (Through natural selection, people who have acquired disease-resistant genes are more likely to survive.)

In the Americas, however, there were only a few domesticated animals, which did not carry harmful germs, so the transference of disease from animals to humans was unlikely. In fact, the Americas were considered virtually disease-free. Since North and South America had no exposure to European diseases, severe outbreaks of disease were destined to occur once the newcomers arrived. We will probably never know how many people died as a result of the Europeans' arrival in the Americas.

Captain George Weymouth kidnapped several Indians in the area, among them Tisquantum, who later became known to the English settlers at Plymouth colony as Squanto. Squanto was a member of the Patuxet tribe, whose lands centered around the area that became Plymouth.

By the time the English colonists reached New England in 1620, however, the Patuxets had all been killed by diseases brought to the colonies on English ships. Only Squanto was left. He would prove to be a good friend to the English settlers.

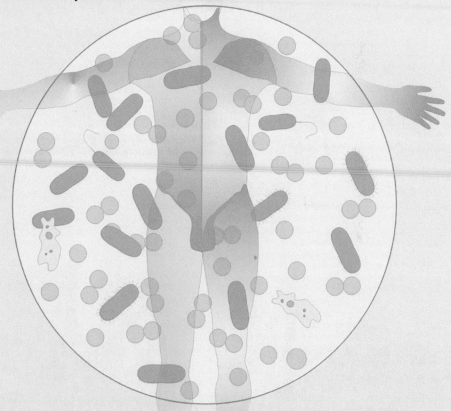

Germs killed more Native Americans than any weapon.

21

Mayflower

Two
THE PLYMOUTH COLONY

The landing party pushed the little boat away from the side of the *Mayflower*. After sixty-five days at sea, they were eager to find a place to establish their new colony. Nothing had gone quite as they had intended from the time they had left the Netherlands. First, their second ship, the *Speedwell*, had developed a leak and delayed the start of the voyage by a month. The *Speedwell* could not be repaired, and they had to leave it behind, crowding everyone who still wanted to come onto the *Mayflower*.

The colonists' original patent had given them the right to settle in Virginia, around the mouth of the Hudson River, near Long Island. The voyage across the Atlantic was terrible, so stormy that one of the main beams of the ship cracked. The colonists fixed the beam with a huge iron screw they had brought along for a printing press, but they knew they needed to reach land soon. By the time the colonists sighted North America, November had arrived. They put ashore, despite the fact they were several hundred miles north of their intended destination; the weather and the condition of their ship made it impossible to continue on any further. On November 21, 1620, Myles Standish led a small group of men ashore to search for a good place to settle.

THE NORTHERN COLONIES

Pilgrims *are people who journey to foreign lands.*

After such a long and dangerous journey, the ***Pilgrims***—as those who arrived on the *Mayflower* were later called—fell on their knees and blessed God for bringing them safely to America. Their travels had taken them from Scrooby in England to the Netherlands, and now to a home of their own in their "New World." God and religion were very important in the lives of the Pilgrims. In many ways, their religious beliefs were similar to those of the Puritans back in England. Both groups

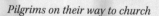

Pilgrims on their way to church

believed the Church of England needed purification, a simplification that got rid of "Catholic" rituals. They believed each person was individually responsible to God and should talk to him directly, not through a priest or spiritual leader. Reading the Bible and obeying its commands were key in both Puritan and Pilgrim society.

The Pilgrims also believed hard work honored God and that he would bless it. This idea often led to the assumption that wealthy people in their society were also very holy people, since God had blessed them so much. This may seem arrogant, but the Pilgrims needed their belief in hard work to survive in Plymouth colony.

They had arrived in New England with the winter storms, and they had to construct houses quickly. Each man built his own house, but first, they worked together to erect a common house. Until the common house had been completed, everyone slept on board the *Mayflower*.

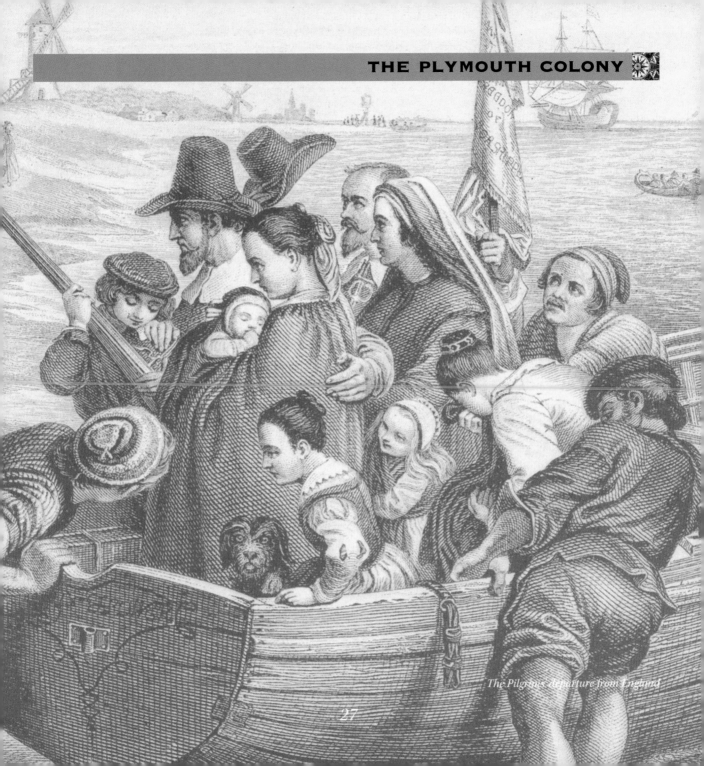

The Pilgrims' departure from England

27

Squanto, the Pilgrims' Friend

In 1614, Squanto was kidnapped and taken to England. Before that he had lived in Patuxet, where the Pilgrims built Plymouth. When he returned to his home, he found his entire tribe had died from a disease carried by one of the English sailors.

The work on the common house went slowly. Many of the colonists fell ill, exhausted and malnourished after their long voyage on the *Mayflower*. Snow and cold also interfered with the work. The first building in Plymouth—the common house—was finally finished in January 1621, nearly two months after their arrival.

Many people died during that first winter in America. By the time warmer weather arrived in March, only fifty-two of the 102 people who had arrived on the *Mayflower* still lived, and a mere seven people remained healthy for the entire winter. These seven had the exhausting job of

Squanto's arrival

Massasoit's treaty with the Pilgrims

Squanto also helped the Plymouth colonists learn how to live in their new home. He showed them how to use herring as fertilizer on their fields, showed them which berries and roots could be eaten, and hunted with them in the woods. The Plymouth colonists owed their survival over the next few years to the help of Squanto and the local Wampanoag Indians.

looking after all the others and burying the dead.

On March 16, 1621, an Indian suddenly walked into the colony. Samoset, an Indian from Maine, had learned some English from fishermen and was able to communicate with the Pilgrims. Samoset soon gained the trust of the colonists, and when he returned a week later, he brought with him several of the local Indians, including Tisquantum, whom the Pilgrims called Squanto.

With the help of Samoset and Squanto, the Pilgrims were able to make a peace treaty with Massasoit, leader of the Wampanoag Indians.

Samoset and the Pilgrims

That fall, the Pilgrims celebrated the harvest of their first crops in their new home with a festival. This festival became known as the first Thanksgiving, although the Pilgrims did not call their celebration Thanksgiving. The party lasted for three days. Ninety Indian men visited Plymouth for the harvest gathering, including Massasoit. Food overflowed the tables, cooked by the four married women and five teenage girls remaining in the colony. The Pilgrims and Indians ran races and played games together. Through this harvest celebration, the friendships between the colonists and the Indians grew stronger. For the next fifty years, the

The Pilgrims first Thanksgiving

colonists had a peaceful and friendly relationship with the Native people.

Their ***alliance*** with the Indians made life simpler for the Pilgrims. They could trade with the Wampanoag, and they did not have to worry so much about raids and attacks from other Indians.

Many of the colonists also contributed a great deal to the settlement's survival. One of these, Myles Standish, was not a member of the original Separatist group. Standish came from a wealthy family in Northern England and had fought with the English in the Netherlands against Spain. While in the Netherlands, he had met the English ***congregation*** of Separatists. When the congregation

*An **alliance** is a partnership that is beneficial to all parties.*

*A **congregation** is a group of worshippers.*

31

The signing of the Mayflower Compact

ing herein their true love unto their friends and brethren; a rare example and worthy to be remembered.

Standish was a short man with a fierce temper. He became close friends with one of the Indians, Hobomok, a warrior. In 1622, he went with Hobomok and a group of men to rescue a Wampanoag Indian village under attack by an enemy tribe. During the fight, Standish killed several Indians, including one who insulted his height. When John Robinson, the Separatists' pastor who had remained in the Netherlands, heard about the incident, he condemned Standish as violent and hot-tempered and advised the colonists not to follow him. Despite

decided to emigrate to the New World, they hired Standish as their Military Captain.

Myles Standish was one of the seven people who did not get sick at all during the first winter at Plymouth. William Bradford, the governor of the colony, wrote that Standish and the other healthy colonists:

spared no pains night nor day, but with abundance of toil and hazard of their own health, fetched them [the sick] wood, made them fires, dressed them meat, made their beds, washed their loathsome clothes, clothed and unclothed them. In a word, did all the homely and necessary offices for them which dainty and queasy stomachs cannot endure to be named; and all this willingly and cheerfully, without any grudging in the least, show-

The Mayflower Compact

The Mayflower Compact

When the Pilgrims left for America they had an agreement with the Virginia Company to settle in Virginia. Instead, they landed in New England and decided to settle there. This meant they would not be governed by the laws of the Virginia Company. Before they disembarked from the Mayflower, they drafted and signed the Mayflower Compact in which they agreed to govern themselves:

In the name of God, Amen. We whose names are under-written, the loyal subjects of our dread sovereign Lord, King James, by the grace of God, of Great Britain, France, and Ireland King, Defender of the Faith, etc.

Having undertaken, for the glory of God, and advancement of the Christian faith, and honor of our King and Country, a voyage to plant the first colony in the northern parts of Virginia, do by these presents solemnly and mutually, in the presence of God, and one of another, covenant and combine our selves together into a civil body politic, for our better ordering and preservation and furtherance of the ends aforesaid; and by virtue hereof to enact, constitute, and frame such just and equal laws, ordinances, acts, constitutions and offices, from time to time, as shall be thought most meet and convenient for the general good of the Colony, unto which we promise all due submission and obedience. In witness whereof we have hereunder subscribed our names at Cape Cod, the eleventh of November, in the year of the reign of our sovereign lord, King James, of England, France, and Ireland, the eighteenth, and of Scotland the fifty-fourth. Anno Dom. 1620.

Unanimously *means every-one is in agreement.*

A
DESCRIPTION
of *New England*:
OR
THE OBSERVATIONS, AND
discoueries, of Captain *Iohn Smith* (Admirall of that Country) in the North of *America*, in the year of our *Lord* 1614: with the *succeſſe* of *ſixe Ships*, that went the next yeare 1615 ; and the accidents befell him among the French men of warre:

With the proofe of the preſent benefit this Countrey affoords: whither this preſent yeare, 1616, eight *voluntary Ships* are gone to make further tryall.

At LONDON
Printed by *Humfrey Lownes*, for *Robert Clerke* ; and are to be ſould at his houſe called the Lodge, in Chancery lane, ouer againſt Lin-colnes Inne. 1616.

First use of the term "New England,"
John Smith, 1616

this, Standish remained a valued and respected member of Plymouth society.

William Bradford, Plymouth's governor, was another of the colony's most influential residents. Bradford had been a part of the original Separatist congregation in Scrooby. In the spring of 1621, the original Plymouth governor died, and the other Pilgrims **unanimously** elected Bradford as his replacement. For the next thirty years, Bradford served as governor of the colony. Much of what is known about the early years of Plymouth comes from Bradford's handwritten journal, *Of Plymouth Colony*. Bradford's writings also give us the name "Pilgrims," from his comment that the Separatists leaving the Netherlands "knew they were pilgrims."

As the Plymouth colony grew, and more ships arrived carrying new colonists, groups began to break off and form new settlements. Bradford found the breakup of the original colony very sad; they had been a tightly knit group, but now many lived too far away to even attend church in Plymouth. As the colonists spread out into the New World, the English presence in New England grew more secure. The arrival of other groups only served to strengthen this foothold.

Treaty of 1621 between the Plymouth Colonists and the Wampanoag Indians

[The people referred to specifically in this treaty are John Carver, the first governor of Plymouth, and Massasoit, chief of the Wampanoag. Each "he" and "theirs" refers to both Carver and Massasoit.]

1. That he nor any of his should do hurt to any of their people.

2. That if any of his did hurt any of theirs, he should send the offender, that they might punish him.

3. That if anything were taken away from any of theirs, he should cause it to be restored; and they should do the like to his.

4. If any did unjustly war against him, they would aid him; if any did war against them, he should aid them.

5. He should send to his neighbors confederates to certify them of this, that they might not wrong them, but might be likewise compromised in the conditions of peace.

6. That when their men came to them, they should leave their bows and arrows behind them.

7. That King James would esteem Massasoit as his friend and ally.

Three
THE MASSACHUSETTS BAY COLONY

In 1625, after only a few months as King of England, Charles I married the French princess Henrietta Marie de Bourbon, a Roman Catholic. Earlier, Charles had promised Parliament that even if he married a Roman Catholic, he would not change any of the laws requiring people to attend Anglican Church services. Now, however, he agreed, as part of the marriage treaty with France, not to persecute English Catholics for refusing to attend Anglican services. Parliament, which consisted mainly of Puritans, was angry with Charles for breaking his promise to them, and they also worried that more changes might come, favoring Roman Catholics even further.

When the Puritan movement began toward the end of the 1500s, most Puritans believed the Anglican Church could be reformed from within. Only a few Separatists left the church altogether. One group of these Separatists had **founded** Plymouth Colony in 1620. With the changes Charles I began making, however, some Puritans began doubting their original idea of reforming the church from within. Rather than reform, England was beginning to move farther away from Puritan *ideals*. Besides his

Founded means formally established.

Ideals are standards or principles to which people aspire.

*A **charter** is a formal agreement authorizing the establishment of a new organization or granting rights and privileges to a person or existing organization.*

friendships with Catholic nations, Charles I spent large amounts of money on the arts, which many Puritans considered wasteful.

One group of Puritan businessmen developed a plan for colonizing the New World. In their presentation to King Charles seeking permission to settle in America, the men introduced the idea as a way for the English crown to earn money. Charles liked the idea and granted the Massachusetts Bay Company a **charter** to settle in New England.

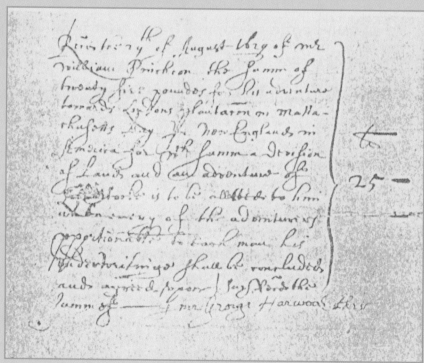

An original share in the Massachusetts Bay Company

John Winthrop

Winthrop Fleet—left England and made the long trip across the Atlantic to New England. In early summer, the Puritans landed in Massachusetts and founded Boston and several villages around it.

One of the ships, the *Arbella*, carried John Winthrop, the new governor. Before leaving England, Winthrop preached the now-famous "City on a Hill" sermon to his fellow colonists. Winthrop called the sermon "A Model of Christian Charity" and in it described God's purpose for the about-to-be-settled New England colony. The colony was to be a Christian community, founded on virtues such as love, kindness, and purity. The new colony would be an example to the world: "For we must consider that we shall be as a City upon a hill. The eyes of all people are upon us."

John Winthrop had served as a justice of the peace in England before traveling with the Massachusetts Bay Company to New England. He had become a devout Puritan and believed England would soon be judged by God for its corruption. Therefore, he thought, all true Christians should leave England. This idea inspired large numbers of Puritan emigrants to travel to New England.

In 1628 and 1629, the company sent out two small groups, founding colonies on Cape Ann and Salem, Massachusetts. In 1629, King Charles disbanded Parliament, and suddenly many more Puritans decided they wanted to leave England. In 1630, a fleet of eleven ships carrying seven hundred passengers—called the

Nonconsecutive *means not following one after another without an interruption.*

Heresy *refers to holding a belief that does not agree with established religion.*

Repressive *means to have strict control over something.*

Theology *is the study of religion.*

In his position as governor, Winthrop was a fair man. Over the next twenty years, he served as governor for twelve **nonconsecutive** terms. He tried hard to live up to his own ideals about what a Christian should act like, and he worked hard to shape the Massachusetts Bay Colony into what he believed a Christian community should look like as well. Although Winthrop would seem very strict to Americans today, he was much less rigid than many Puritans of his day. He did not execute as many people for **heresy** as did other governors, and he tried to limit some of the more **repressive** ideas, such as requiring women to wear veils in church.

Politics and religion could not be separated in the Massachusetts Bay Colony. To have a part in the governing of the colony or even to vote, colonists needed to be church members. Religious leaders closely controlled who could become a member of the church. However, the Puritans did make sure members of the clergy could not become government leaders. They feared giving too much power to the clergy, since in England this had led to abuses of power.

An early scandal in the Massachusetts Bay Colony involved a woman named Anne Hutchinson. Anne had immigrated to the colony in 1634 with her husband Will and their fifteen children. As a child, Anne had seen her father jailed for his outspoken Puritan ideas. She had read the books in her father's library and become very interested in *theology*. Her upbringing gave her a good education and an

Boston harbor

Conviction *means found guilty of an illegal act.*

Banished *means made to leave a place.*

Anne Hutchinson's meetings

Anne Hutchinson

that would happen and therefore people should make no effort to try to change events or other people. Preaching accomplished nothing, and it did not matter if people obeyed the Bible or not.

The Puritan leaders were shocked when they discovered what Anne had been talking about in her women's group. In 1638, Anne was arrested, tried for heresy, and, after her *conviction*, *banished* from the colony.

Anne and her family, along with a small group of followers, left Massachusetts Bay and moved south. For a little while, they lived in the Rhode Island area, but then, after her husband died, Anne moved south again to Long Island. In September 1643, Anne and five of her children were killed in an Indian attack.

Some in the Massachusetts Bay Colony thought Anne's fate was a judgment from God, while others were shocked and saddened. A few had agreed with Anne's teachings but had been afraid to speak out.

Although Massachusetts Bay had been founded on religious ideals, that did not mean everyone agreed on the details of those ideals. Anne Hutchinson was not the first to leave the colony because of religious differences, nor would she be the last.

awareness that sometimes a person suffered for his or her beliefs.

In New England, Anne began holding a women's group in her home to discuss the Bible and Christianity. The community leaders approved of such meetings to a certain extent, but Anne began to use the group to talk about her own ideas. Anne believed God knew everything

yͤ most vnworthy Svant
Roger Wjlliams

Four
RHODE ISLAND

The little church in Salem, Massachusetts, became the center of **controversy** in 1634 when their pastor died and the unofficial assistant pastor, Roger Williams, replaced him. Williams had always been a controversial and outspoken figure. Since he had arrived in New England in 1631, he had stirred up trouble for the Massachusetts Bay governors, criticizing them for keeping too close ties with the Church of England.

Williams had spent time in Plymouth Colony and among the Indians, learning their language. Earlier, he had refused to pastor a Massachusetts church because he disapproved of the colony's connections with the Anglican Church. Salem, however, had more Separatist ideals than the rest of the colony. When Williams accepted the Salem leaders' offer to **pastor** their church, the controversy began again.

Controversy *means a disagreement.*

To **pastor** *means to minister to.*

Williams immediately condemned the Massachusetts Bay Charter, because it referred to the king as Christian. Williams believed the Church of England had become thoroughly corrupted, and the king, he thought, was anything but Christian. Another problem Williams had with the leadership of Massachusetts Bay was their requirement of oaths. The colonists had sworn oaths of loyalty to the king before they received their charter to establish a colony. Once in New England, the governors of the colony required the colonists to swear oaths of loyalty to the colony government. Williams disagreed with the whole idea of oaths. He believed no one could require such an oath except Jesus Christ.

Problems intensified over a conflict concerning a piece of land claimed by both Salem and the Massachusetts Bay court. The court agreed to let Salem have the land, but only if they got rid of Roger Williams. At first, the church, with the strong encouragement of Williams, defied the order. Eventually, however, Salem received so much pressure from Massachusetts Bay they felt they had no choice but to fire Williams.

In October 1635, Williams was banished entirely from the Massachusetts Bay Colony. The colony leaders

Providence, Rhode Island

46

intended to send Williams back to England. Williams, hearing of the plan, disappeared into the wilderness and lived with the Indians.

In June 1636, Williams arrived in Rhode Island. From the local Indians, he purchased some land to establish a colony there. A handful of colonists from the Massachusetts Bay area had come with him to Rhode Island, and together they founded Providence, named for God's blessings.

In 1643, Williams returned to England and received a charter from the king for the new colony. One of the most unique things about Rhode Island was its religious freedom. Other New England colonies were built on the principle of religious freedom as well, but they meant freedom for their own kind of worship, not for those who disagreed with

Roger Williams' landing site on Rhode Island

47

them. Rhode Island, on the other hand, accepted Baptists, Catholics, Quakers, and Jews—whoever wanted to come.

Since it would let anyone live there, Rhode Island acquired a bad reputation among the other colonies. Soon after its founding, someone asked where a boatload of Quakers had gone after they had been turned away from another colony. A clergyman answered, "We suppose they went to Rhode Island, for that is the receptacle of all sorts of riff-raff people and is nothing less than the sewer of New England. All of the cranks retire thither. They are not tolerated in any other place."

Another thing that made Rhode Island unique was its friendly relationship with Native Americans. The Plymouth Colony had started with good relations with the Indians as well, but the friendship lasted only as long as it was convenient for the European settlers. Small, struggling colonies found it easier to befriend the Indians than did larger, growing settlements. When colonies were small, the people needed the help of the Indians to survive. As colonies grew larger, however, people wanted Indian land for themselves.

Roger Williams respected the Indians as fellow human beings. Earlier, he had upset the leaders of the Massachusetts Bay Colony by condemning them for taking Indian land without any thought for the people who lived on it. During his time with the Indians shortly after his arrival in New England, Williams studied Native languages, and later, he wrote a book called *Key into the Language of America*. Not only did the book include guidelines on translating Indian languages, but it also contained tips on peaceful communication.

In 1675, when Williams was an old man, King Philip's War began. King Philip was the English name for Metacomet, the son of Massasoit who had befriended the Pilgrims in Plymouth. The Indians were tired of seeing the English settlers take their lands, and fighting broke out between settlers and bands of Indians all along the New England coast.

For a long time, no Indians attacked Providence. They knew Roger Williams lived there, and they respected him as a good and honorable man. Finally, however, a group of Indians arrived to burn the town. Williams walked out to meet the attackers by himself, carrying no weapons. Despite his arguments, the Indians told him Providence would have to

Roger Williams and Native Americans

King Philip

be burned. Williams himself, though, would remain unharmed.

After the English conquered the Indians in King Philip's War—partly through alliance with other Indian tribes—Providence was rebuilt, along with the other towns that had been destroyed. Roger Williams lived until 1684. He saw his colony rebuilt before his death.

Throughout its early history, Rhode Island became known as a place of religious freedom. Roger Williams firmly believed that each person should be allowed to worship God (or not wor-

ship God) as their own conscience prompted. He believed it was wrong to force someone to attend a particular church or agree to a certain belief. In his book *The Bloody Tenet of Persecution for Cause of Conscience*, Williams wrote, "It is the will and command of God, that . . . a permission of the most Paganish, Jewish, Turkish, or Antichristian consciences and worships, be granted to all men, in all nations." Williams truly believed this and succeeded in making Rhode Island a place where people of all religions were welcomed.

Roger Williams' will

Thomas Hooker

Five
CONNECTICUT

On a June morning in 1636, the sun shone brightly on a large group of men, women, and children walking slowly across a grassy hilltop. One woman rested on a *litter* carried by two men. Around the group, cows chewed mouthfuls of grass; the cattle slowly moved forward as boys flicked at them with thin branches.

The group walked for a hundred miles: through forests, across swamps, over hills. They followed Reverend Thomas Hooker from Massachusetts to Connecticut, where they founded the new town of Hartford. Hooker's wife was too sick to walk, so the other members of the group carried her.

Thomas Hooker had arrived in the Massachusetts Bay Colony in 1633 and immediately begun serving as a pastor. He had grown up a Puritan and discovered early on he did not fit in with the Church of England. When he came to Massachusetts, he found he did not fit in there either.

Hooker clashed with the other Massachusetts Bay pastors and leaders because of his views on democracy. He believed all men

*A **litter** is a stretcher used to carry a person.*

should be allowed to vote, while other Massachusetts Bay leaders wanted to allow men to vote only if they owned property and were members of the church. After a while, these differences made Hooker so unhappy he asked to be allowed to move south and start another colony.

The Massachusetts Bay leaders did not want to let Hooker leave. He was a good pastor, even if they did not agree with all his ideas. Hooker persisted, though, and in June 1636 he left Massachusetts Bay with about a hundred people. Most of their belongings traveled by sea south to Connecticut, but Hooker and his

Thomas Hooker on his way to Connecticut

friends walked, driving the cattle along beside them. Two weeks later, they reached the Connecticut River and began to build the town of Hartford.

Hooker's main reasons for leaving Massachusetts were religious, not political. Like the other Puritans, he wanted to build the ideal Christian community. He believed the Massachusetts Bay Colony was wrong not to allow all men to vote, regardless of church membership or property ownership. Therefore, he wanted to found a community where this mistake was corrected, and all men would be allowed to take part in government. (Women, of course, would not be granted the right to vote for more than two hundred years.)

In the spring of 1638, men from the growing towns along the Connecticut River—Hartford, Windsor, and Wethersfied—met at Hartford to form a General Court governing the area. Reverend Hooker preached a sermon at the court's opening session, saying, "The foundation of authority is laid in the free consent of the people. . . . As God has given us liberty let us take it."

This sermon inspired the creation of the Fundamental Orders, a *constitution* of sorts setting out the governing of Connecticut. The Fundamental Orders stressed the rights of the individual and created Connecticut as a *commonwealth*. On January 14, 1639, the General Court of Connecticut approved the Fundamental Orders and they went into effect.

In 1637, another group of Puritans traveled from the Netherlands, where they had been living, to England, and then on to America. Reverend John Davenport led the five hundred

*A **constitution** is a written set of rules to govern a settlement.*

*A **commonwealth** is a self-governing territory.*

55

The Fundamental Orders of Connecticut (January 14, 1639)

The preamble of the Fundamental Orders, the governing charter of the Connecticut River towns, acknowledged the need for laws to order their society:

For as much as it hath pleased Almighty God by the wise disposition of his divine providence so to order and dispose of things that we the Inhabitants and Residents of Windsor, Hartford and Wethersfield are now cohabiting and dwelling in and upon the River of Connectecotte and the lands thereunto adjoining; and well knowing where a people are gathered together the word of God requires that to maintain the peace and union of such a people there should be an orderly and decent Government established according to God, to order and dispose of the affairs of the people at all seasons as occasion shall require; do therefore associate and conjoin ourselves to be as one Public State or Commonwealth; and do for ourselves and our successors and such as shall be adjoined to us at any time hereafter, enter into Combination and Confederation together, to maintain and preserve the liberty and purity of the Gospel of our Lord Jesus which we now profess, as also, the discipline of the Churches, which according to the truth of the said Gospel is now practiced amongst us; as also in our civil affairs to be guided and governed according to such Laws, Rules, Orders and Decrees as shall be made, ordered, and decreed as followeth.

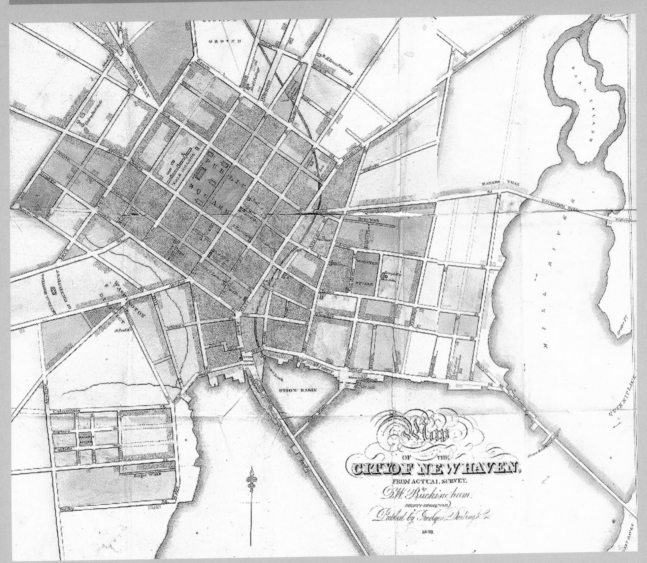

Map of New Haven

*A **monarchy** is a country ruled by a king or queen.*

*When something is **restored**, it is returned to its previous form.*

King Charles II

Puritans, joined in London by the merchant Theophilus Eaton. At first, the group went to the Massachusetts Bay Colony to settle, but they felt uneasy there, believing the colony did not follow religious guidelines that were as strict as they would have liked.

On April 24, 1638, Reverend Davenport and his congregation arrived in Connecticut and began building the town of New Haven. Again, this group wanted to create the perfect Christian community. They also wanted to create a trading empire along the Atlantic coast, dealing in furs and fish.

New Haven's dream of commercial success was never realized. Most of the trading ships traveled to Boston, a more established port. Finally New Haven got their own ship. They loaded it with their harvested crops and sent it off to England. The ship was never heard from again; presumably, it was lost at sea.

New Haven remained independent from Hartford and its surrounding towns for several years. In 1639, they adopted

Reverend John Davenport

Duke of York

their own set of Fundament Articles, similar to the Connecticut River towns' Fundamental Orders.

Meanwhile, back in England, Parliament had arrested King Charles I in 1649, and had him beheaded. For eleven years, Parliament ruled England. Then, in 1660, the **monarchy** was **restored** and Charles's son became King Charles II. Charles II wanted revenge on the men who had executed his father. Three of the men who had signed the execution order fled to New Haven, Connecticut, and Reverend Davenport hid them in a cave there.

Four years later, the Duke of York, brother of Charles II, attacked and captured nearby New Amsterdam. The leaders of New Haven worried that the duke, a Catholic, would soon capture their city as well. Unwilling to submit to possible Catholic rule, New Haven agreed to join with the other Connecticut towns and give up its independence. For the next hundred years, until 1873, New Haven would serve as co-capitol of Connecticut, along with Hartford.

Six
NEW NETHERLAND

The countries of Europe wanted the wealth of the East. Merchants dreamed of an easy sea route to Asia, through North America or north through the Arctic. The only sea routes available at the time took them far to the south and around either Africa or South America; both routes were long and dangerous. Explorer after explorer searched for the Northwest Passage, only to fail as possible routes dwindled into narrow rivers or ran up against thick pack ice.

The explorer Henry Hudson wanted desperately to find the Northwest Passage. After two failed attempts, though, the Muscovy Company he worked for in England decided to spend their money elsewhere. Then, at the end of 1608, the Dutch East India Company hired Hudson to lead its own *expedition* in search of the Northwest Passage.

*An **expedition** is an organized trip to explore an unknown territory.*

HALF MOON

The Half Moon, Henry Hudson's ship

The Dutch wanted Hudson to sail north, but he had already been north twice. He knew the ice-choked waters of the Arctic would probably never make a good trade route. Instead of north, in the early summer of 1609, Henry Hudson sailed west toward the "New World."

After exploring along the coast of North America, Hudson sailed into New York

Henry Hudson

harbor in early September and began to make his way up the wide river that would eventually bear his name. A week and a half later, having sailed 150 miles upriver, Hudson realized the river was not the Northwest Passage he sought. He had reached the area just north of present-day Albany, but his scouts told him that up ahead the river grew so shallow it was only seven feet deep. His ship, the *Half Moon*, kept running aground, and Hudson decided they would have to turn back.

Hudson reached England in November, but before he could continue on to Amsterdam to report to his employers, English officials arrested him for working for a foreign country. The ship continued on to the Netherlands without Hudson, carrying with it all the notes and journals he had written on the voyage.

The Dutch were annoyed with Hudson for not listening to them and traveling north. They thought maybe he wanted them to fail, because he wanted the English to succeed in finding the Northwest Passage first. This did not stop them from sending trade ships to the area Hudson

Guilders were worth approximately 40 U.S. cents, or .45 euro.

Recruited means enlisted someone for a particular purpose.

had explored. In 1623, another company—the Dutch West India Company—named the region New Netherland and built a trading fort called Fort Orange near where Albany is today.

The next year, ships of settlers began arriving in New Netherland, traveling to Fort Orange and several other Dutch settlements. Many of the first settlers were not Dutch but Walloon, from part of Belgium, fleeing Spanish occupation of their country.

Before long, the settlers in the northern settlements around Fort Orange faced Indian attacks, caught in the middle of a war between the Mohawk and the Mahican tribes. In 1626, Peter Minuit, the Director General of the Dutch West India Company, purchased the island of Manhattan from the Indians with goods worth about 60 *guilders*. The northern colonists moved back downriver and settled on Manhattan, naming their town New Amsterdam.

The Dutch West India Company had founded New Netherland to make money. They discovered, however, that by the time they built their forts and paid all the soldiers, doctors, and craftsmen they *recruited* to settle in their colony, there was not much money left over as profit. In 1628, they came up with a plan they hoped would increase both their profits and the number of settlers.

The Patroonship plan would give a patroon—a landowner—a large piece of land to live on as a governing lord. In return, the patroon would pay to bring over a certain number of settlers to live there. Most people did not like the

Peter Minuit

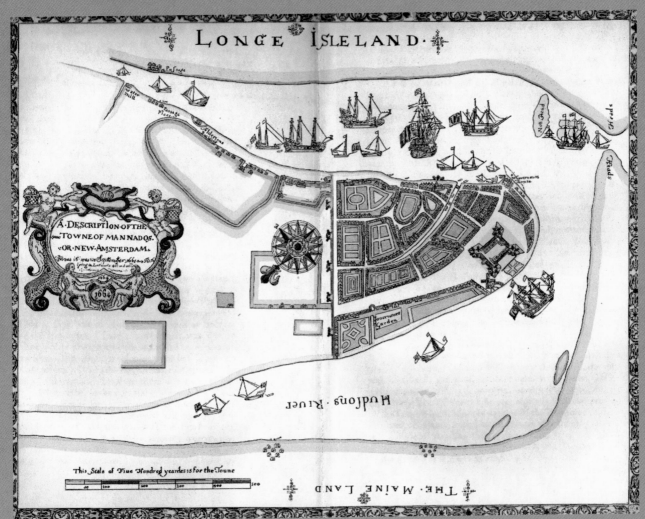

Map of Manhattan, 1661

Patroonship plan, though. Under the plan, the Dutch West India Company would keep all the fishing and fur trading rights. Potential patroons thought trade would have been the only reason to accept the plan.

The next year, the company revised the plan, giving patroons larger pieces of land, less strict colonization requirements, and the right to trade on their own. In 1630, Kiliaen van Rensselear became patroon to a large area near Fort Orange, which he named Rensselaerswyck. Other patroons soon followed.

In 1647, Peter Stuyvesant, the new Director General of the Dutch West India Company, arrived in New Amsterdam. Stuyvesant had earlier served as governor of Curacao in the Caribbean, where he had lost his right leg during an attack on a neighboring Portuguese island. His wooden leg, decorated with silver nails, earned him the nickname "Peg Leg Pete" and "Old Silver Nails."

Almost as soon as he arrived on Manhattan, Stuyvesant started making changes that annoyed the New Netherland residents. He raised taxes, enforced strict Sunday observances, and outlawed selling alcohol and firearms to the Indians. The merchants were angry; they wanted more control of their government, not less.

Finally, Stuyvesant agreed to set up a town government in New Amsterdam, hoping to **appease** the residents. Despite this gesture, he continued to rule the entire colony himself.

One of the jobs the company had given Stuyvesant was to increase the colony's defenses and end the conflicts with the Indians. In 1649, he traveled to Fort Orange and ordered

Peter Stuyvesant

*To **appease** means to pacify.*

The Dutch colony of New Netherland

that certain houses be torn down to make the fort easier to defend. The residents did not like this idea, and the patroon refused to obey Stuyvesant's orders. Stuyvesant then sent a group of soldiers to make sure the houses really were torn down.

Peter Stuyvesant's signature

67

In 1650, the patroons of New Netherland sent a letter to the leaders of the Dutch West India Company in Europe, telling them about the condition of the colony. The company ordered Stuyvesant to return to Holland and discuss the situation in person. Stuyvesant refused to go, however, and no actions were ever taken against him.

As the Dutch colony of New Netherland grew, so did the English colonies that bordered them to the north and south. In 1660, Charles II became king of England after the restoration of the monarchy. Soon, Charles began thinking about his North American colonies and how England owned almost all the East Coast. Charles thought England needed to close the geographic gap created by New Netherland.

On August 27, 1664, the English navy launched an attack on New Amsterdam. King Charles had given the area to his brother, the Duke of York, but the duke had to take the land from the Dutch before he could occupy it.

When the English captain sent a letter to Stuyvesant asking for his surrender, Stuyvesant angrily tore it into pieces. The town leaders pleaded with him not to allow bloodshed, and Stuyvesant at last agreed. On September 9, 1664, he signed a treaty giving control of the colony to the

"New York Narrows" by Augustus Kollner

English. The town leaders proclaimed the English captain governor and renamed their city New York.

The Dutch did not want to give up their North American colony so easily. The takeover of New Netherland by the English triggered a two-year war between the two nations. Finally, the Dutch agreed to let the English keep New Netherland in return for the colony of Surinam in South America. Even then, the conflicts con-tinued. In 1673, the Dutch briefly retook what was now New York. The Treaty of Westminster on November 10, 1674, at last gave England final control over the colony.

The Dutch control over New York lasted barely fifty years, but it left a lasting impression. From numerous place names along the Hudson River to cultural contributions such as Easter eggs, waffles, bowling and skating, the Dutch impact on New York State lives on.

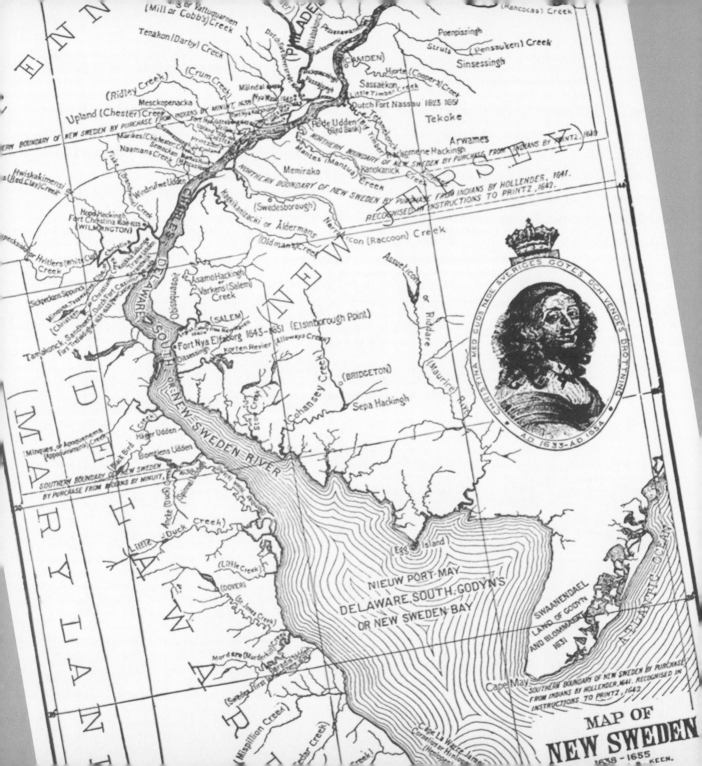

MAP OF
NEW SWEDEN
1638 - 1655

Seven
NEW SWEDEN

In the middle of the 1600s, Sweden owned all of what is now Finland and part of Norway, Russia, Poland, Latvia, Estonia, Lithuania, and Germany; Sweden numbered among the great powers of Europe. In 1637, Swedish merchants formed the New Sweden Company, together with a few German and Dutch merchants. They intended to establish a colony for trading along the coast of North America in an area not already inhabited by the English or Dutch.

To lead the expedition, the New Sweden Company hired Peter Minuit. Minuit had earlier served as the governor of New Netherland and helped to purchase Manhattan Island. He had familiarity with the types of difficulties faced by colonies in the North American wilderness, and the inexperienced New Sweden Company wanted his first-hand knowledge of the area.

In March 1638, two ships, the *Kalmar Nyckel* and the *Fogel Grip*, arrived in Delaware Bay carrying fifty settlers. Landing at the location of present-day Wilmington, Delaware, the colonists began building a fort. They named it Fort Christina, after Sweden's twelve-year-old queen.

At first, the New Sweden Company had trouble recruiting people to travel to their North American colony. Most people did not seem to

Tactical *refers to military strategy.*

A **duty** *is a tax.*

Treason *is betrayal of one's country.*

Sweden's flag

be interested in leaving their homes for the danger of the "New World." Unlike the New England colonists, they did not face religious persecution at home, and the possibilities for profit seemed too small to be enticing.

To build the population of the New Sweden Colony, the company looked for married soldiers who had been charged with various crimes. Then, the company offered to send the soldiers and their families to North America as an alternative to spending time in prison. By 1655, the New Sweden Company had sent six hundred people to their colony. As the colony grew, farms and small communities spread out along the Delaware River and throughout parts of what are now Delaware, New Jersey, Pennsylvania, and Maryland.

From 1643 to 1653, Johan Printz served as governor of the New Sweden Colony. Printz had not wanted to be governor of New Sweden. He had served in the Swedish military until a **tactical** error during the Thirty Years' War cost him his position. Then, in 1642, he was appointed governor of New Sweden. The New Sweden Company told him he would serve as governor for three years and then he could come home. After three years, however, the company told Printz they could find no one to take over as governor. He would have to stay on.

Despite his reluctance to be there, Printz did his best at his job. He increased the colony's defenses and built Fort Elfsborg near present-day Salem, New Jersey. The fort served as added protection against Dutch and English ships, since enemy ships would

Johan Printz

Delaware Bay. The Dutch built Fort Casimir at present-day New Castle, Delaware, and forced trading ships to pay a *duty* before they could reach or leave Fort Christina. Stuyvesant ignored both Printz's protests and the copies of land deeds Printz sent proving Sweden owned the land.

Throughout these conflicts, Printz heard nothing from the New Sweden Company, although he wrote them numerous pleas for help. With the Dutch so close now, Fort Elfsborg no longer had as great a purpose and could not be easily reached without passing Dutch-ruled areas. Unhappily, Printz abandoned the fort and focused his attention on Fort Christina.

In 1652, rains ruined many of the crops in New Sweden, and by the summer of 1653, the colonists were miserable. Their food supplies had dwindled, and the nearby Dutch presence worried them. Printz had been ill for most of the year and could not deal with the rising tensions. In the fall of 1653, twenty-two colonists presented Printz with a petition listing their complaints against him. Printz had had enough. He arrested the leader of the group bringing the petition and had him tried and executed for *treason*.

have to pass Fort Elfsborg to reach Fort Christina.

In May of 1651, Printz fought off a Dutch attack led by Peter Stuyvesant. The Dutch retreated, but they did not give up. Shortly afterward, Stuyvesant claimed the Swedish land from just south of Fort Christina down to

Fort Casimir

After that, Printz decided to go to Sweden himself and talk with the company leaders. In 1654, Printz returned to Europe, and the New Sweden Company sent Johan Rising to take his place.

Rising did his best to improve the situation in New Sweden. Soon after his arrival, he captured the Dutch Fort Casimir and renamed it Fort Trinity. He hoped to soon drive the Dutch completely out of New Sweden.

The loss of Fort Casimir enraged Peter Stuyvesant. In the summer of 1655, he sailed up the Delaware River with seven ships and 317 soldiers. Rising had little choice but to surrender first the newly captured Fort Trinity and then, two weeks later, Fort Christina itself.

Stuyvesant's capture of Fort Christina ended the official Swedish presence in North America. Most of the Swedish colonists remained in the area, however, and Stuyvesant even allowed them to organize their own court and govern themselves as a "Swedish nation."

With the English capture of New Netherland in 1664, New Sweden came under English control. Officially, the colony belonged to England after this time, but it continued to enjoy partial self-government until 1682, when the area was included in William Penn's deed to Pennsylvania. With English control the name of the colony also reverted to its earlier name, Delaware, named in honor of the English governor of Virginia, De La Warr, in 1610.

*William Penn as a
young man*

Eight
PENNSYLVANIA AND NEW JERSEY

William Penn was just twelve years old the first time he heard a Quaker minister, Thomas Loe. The sermon intrigued him. His parents, wealthy landowners, belonged to the Anglican Church in England, and Penn had grown up in the Anglican tradition. Quaker views were new and interesting.

The Quakers shared many ideas with the Puritans, who were quite common in England, but the Quakers went even further in their rejection of church rituals and hierarchies. Like the Puritans, Quakers believed individuals could talk directly to God, without the intervention of a priest. Unlike the Puritans, however, they also believed God could speak to anyone personally, even if that person had never read the Bible. They also thought people were naturally good—an idea the Puritans firmly rejected. Quakers did not believe in **ordained** ministers or church buildings. They thought every Christian could be a minister and every house a church. They dressed plainly, considering fancy clothes a distraction.

*To be **ordained** means to be officially appointed a minister by the governing body of a religion.*

Nonorthodox means not following traditional rules or practices.

Something that is *mandatory* is required.

A *proponent* is someone who supports something.

Incentives are things that encourage people to act in a certain way.

When William Penn turned sixteen, he began attending Oxford University. Soon, he was expelled for attending *nonorthodox* prayer meetings and protesting *mandatory* chapel attendance. After finishing his education in France, Penn returned to England, where he encountered the Quaker Thomas Loe again. This time Penn was twenty-three years old, old enough to decide he wanted to become a Quaker.

Over the next fourteen years, Penn became an outspoken *proponent* of Quaker views. He even spent time in prison for breaking religious laws with his preaching and writings.

In 1681, Penn and eleven other Quakers purchased part of New Jersey. Then, Penn approached King Charles II and convinced the king to give him a large piece of land next to New Jersey. The land would be payment for a debt the king had owed Penn's father. Penn called the area Pennsylvania—Penn's woods—after his father, although he worried people would think he had named it after himself.

Penn's original idea involved selling tracts of land for a profit, but he never became rich from the Pennsylvania colony. More important to Penn than the money, however, was the idea that Pennsylvania should be a "holy experiment," where the government would not make laws concerning the religion people should follow. Discussing freedom of religion, Penn wrote, "All men have a natural and infeasible right to worship Almighty God according to the dictates of their own consciences."

In the new colony of Pennsylvania, education was available to all children, the death penalty was only for murder and treason

Title page from work on the persecution of Quakers in New England

78

(unlike England, which gave the death penalty for about two hundred different crimes), and voters could elect the governing council headed by Penn. In 1682, Penn wrote a pamphlet called "Some Account of the Province of Pennsylvania" to attract people to the colony. The pamphlet described the religious freedom the colony offered and gave the prices for land. For 100 pounds, a person could buy a five-thousand-acre lot. Others could rent a two-hundred-acre farm for only a penny an acre.

With all these *incentives*, Penn had no trouble finding settlers. Quakers flocked to the colony, and so did Catholics, Mennonites, Huguenots, and Lutherans. Three thousand came in the first year alone. Seven years later, the population had reached twelve thousand. Many lived in the city of Philadelphia, which Penn designed himself. The city's name meant "the city of brotherly love," and that is what Penn intended it to be. He laid out the streets in a grid, interspersing them with public squares. In his design, he paid close attention to the best layout for fire safety and health concerns.

Just as Quakers believed in freedom from too many church rules, they also believed in laissez-faire government. This meant they thought

First page of Penn's "Frame of Government"

those in charge of governing should step back and not make too many laws restricting the people. Quakers thought people would naturally do the right thing as long as they under-

79

stood the reasons and were not pressured by the government.

This laissez-faire idea translated into extremely low taxes, as well as nonrestrictive laws. The governing council consisted mostly of Quakers, who shared Penn's ideas. The council rarely met, and taxes were hardly ever collected.

Although the people prospered under this system, the colony still needed to pay a yearly fee to the king. Seldom collecting taxes meant the council did not have much money with which to pay this annual fee. When the king's tax collector arrived in Philadelphia one year while Penn was visiting England, the council ignored him.

Penn began to worry that the king would take Pennsylvania away from him if the colony did not start paying the king's tax and obeying English law. To make sure the council followed the law, he hired John Blackwell, an English Anglican, and sent him to Philadelphia.

Blackwell arrived in Philadelphia and found the colony in worse shape than he must have anticipated. Most people seemed happy and prosperous and the colony was peaceful, but nothing got done. The council chamber was dusty and empty. The council president refused to obey any of Blackwell's orders.

Finally, after he had been in Pennsylvania for several months, Blackwell lost his patience. He fired the council president, although none of the council agreed that he had the authority to do so. At one point, Blackwell became so frustrated he took out his sword and threatened to use it on anyone who argued with him further. When he tried to send home the most stubborn council members, all the other members left as well.

William Penn

William Penn with American Indians

Eventually, Blackwell gave up. No matter what he tried, the council continued to quietly resist him.

When Penn heard what had happened, he regretted sending Blackwell. Although he understood Blackwell's position, he humbly asked the council to forgive him.

Throughout his time as governor of Pennsylvania, Penn found himself forced to spend long periods of time in England. Lord

Some Fruits of Solitude

In 1682, William Penn published this little book of sayings anonymously for fear it would lead to charges of treason. Penn covers a wide variety of topics with his "reflections and maxims."

Truth

Where thou art Obliged to speak, be sure speak the Truth: For Equivocation is half way to Lying, as Lying, the whole way to Hell.

Respect

Never esteem any Man, or thy self, the more for Money; nor think the meaner of thy self or another for want of it: Vertue being the just Reason of respecting, and the want of it, of slighting any one.

Of the Rule of Judging

And if Men would once consider one another reasonably, they would either reconcile their Differences, or more Amicably maintain them.

Of State

I love Service, but not State; One is Useful, the other is Superfluous.

The Vain Man

But a Vain Man is a Nauseous Creature: He is so full of himself that he has no Room for any Thing else, be it never so Good or Deserving.

Of Charity

Would God this Divine Virtue were more implanted and diffused among Mankind, the Pretenders to Christianity especially, and we should certainly mind Piety more than Controversy, and Exercise Love and Compassion instead of Censuring and Persecuting one another in any Manner whatsoever.

Baltimore of Maryland claimed that part of Pennsylvania was his by right, and Penn wanted to make sure the king did not decide in favor of Maryland. Once, Penn even heard one of Lord Baltimore's men commenting that Philadelphia was "one of the prettiest towns in Maryland."

Penn was in England when King Charles II died and his younger brother James, the Duke of York, replaced him as king. Penn had been close friends with James, so Penn used the opportunity to have twelve hundred Quakers released from prison.

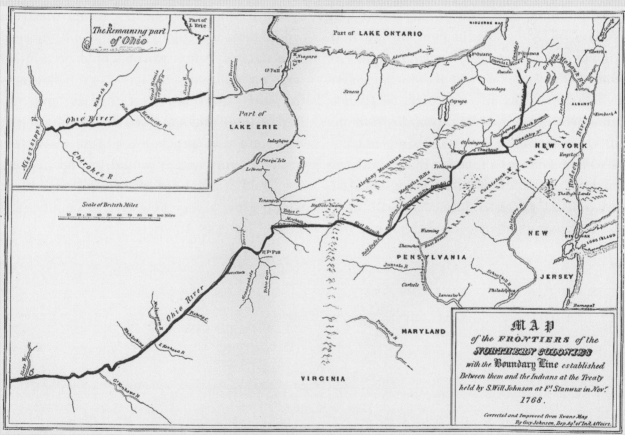

Map of Northern Colonies

But James II was not a popular king. He had too many close ties with Roman Catholics. The people tolerated him, though, until his wife gave birth to a baby boy. Now that James had a legitimate male heir, the potential for a Catholic monarchy was too great to ignore. Secretly, Parliament contacted James's Protestant daughter Mary, the wife of the Dutch king William of Orange. Parliament invited both William and Mary to rule England in place of James. When James learned of the arrangement he feared for his life and fled to France. Parliament considered this an ***abdication*** and quickly replaced him with William and Mary.

William Penn, as a friend of King James, was caught in the middle of the English political situation. Guards arrested him, along with many other supporters of James, and threw him into prison. Eventually, Penn was found innocent of all charges of treason and released, but for a time, between 1692 and 1694, he lost control of Pennsylvania.

William Penn's "holy experiment" did not go as smoothly as he had hoped. And yet, when he first conceived of the idea of Pennsylvania, he wrote to a friend that God would bless the colony and "make it the seed of a nation." Penn's words would be fulfilled nearly a hundred years later, as the delegates for the Continental Congress met in Philadelphia and approved the Declaration of Independence, proclaiming America a free nation. Penn's colony would indeed become the "seed of a nation," and from Penn's ideas would grow a very new sort of county—the United States of America.

The hills of Pennsylvania

Lord Baltimore

Abdication *means the resignation of a sovereign position.*

September 1609 Henry Hudson, working for the Dutch East India Company, discovers the Hudson River while searching for the Northwest Passage.

1603 James I comes to the throne.

1623 The Dutch West India Company founds New Netherland and builds Fort Orange near present-day Albany, New York.

Autumn 1620 The Separatists leave the Netherlands and travel to North America on the *Mayflower*.

Spring 1608 A group of Separatists flees from Scrooby, England to the Netherlands to escape religious persecution.

86

1629 To attract settlers, the Dutch West India Company creates the Patroonship plan, giving landowners a large piece of land and trading rights on that land in return for paying to bring in colonists.

October 1635 Roger Williams is banished from Massachusetts Bay for his strong views on corruption in the Anglican Church and his outspoken condemnation of the oaths required by the colony leaders. He travels to Rhode Island and founds the city of Providence.

1625 Charles I comes to the throne.

1626 Peter Minuit buys the island of Manhattan from the Indians on behalf of the Dutch.

June 1636 Thomas Hooker and a group of one hundred people leave Massachusetts Bay and found the colony of Connecticut, building the city of Hartford.

Early Summer 1630 The Winthrop Fleet, a group of seven hundred Puritans on eleven ships, founds the Massachusetts Bay Colony.

87

March 1638 The New Sweden Company builds Fort Christina, on the site of present-day Wilmington, Delaware.

1638 Anne Hutchinson is banished from Massachusetts Bay for heresy.

1647 Peter Stuyvesant becomes the Director General of the Dutch West India Company and governor of New Netherland.

January 14, 1639 Hartford, Windsor, and Wethersfield approves the Fundamental Orders, a type of constitution for the Commonwealth of Connecticut.

1649 In England, Parliament arrests King Charles I and has him beheaded. For the next eleven years, Parliament rules England in place of the monarchy.

April 24, 1638 John Davenport colonizes New Haven, Connecticut, a separate colony from Hartford and the Connecticut River towns.

Summer 1655 The Dutch, under Peter Stuyvesant, capture New Sweden.

1681 William Penn purchases New Jersey and receives another large piece of land from King Charles II. Penn names his new colony Pennsylvania after his father.

August 27, 1664 The Duke of York attacks New Amsterdam. In September, Peter Stuyvesant signs a treaty giving control of New Netherland to the English.

1660 Charles II becomes king in the restoration of the English monarchy.

1664 The New Haven colony merges with the rest of the Connecticut colony.

THE NORTHERN COLONIES

FURTHER READING

Bjornlund, Lydia. *Massachusetts*. San Diego: Lucent Books, 2002.

Bradford, William and others of the Mayflower Company. H*omes in the Wilderness: A Pilgrim's Journal of Plymouth Plantation in 1620*. 1622. Ed. Margaret Wise Brown. Hamden, Conn.: Linnet Books, 1988.

Collier, Christopher and James Lincoln Collier. *Pilgrims and Puritans: 1620–1676*. Tarrytown, N.Y.: Benchmark Books, 1998.

Daugherty, James. *The Landing of the Pilgrims*. New York: Landmark Books, 1950.

Dean, Ruth and Melissa Thomson. L*ife in the American Colonies*. San Diego: Lucent Books, 1999.

Doherty, Katherine and Craig Doherty. *The Wampanoag*. New York: Franklin Watts, 1995.

Goodnough, David. *The Colony of New York*. New York: Franklin Watts, 1973.

Fradin, Dennis B. *The New York Colony*. Chicago: Children's Press, 1988.

Kline, Andrew A. *Rhode Island*. San Diego: Lucent Books, 2002.

Lukes, Bonnie L. *Colonial America*. San Diego: Lucent Books, 2000.

Morris, Richard B. *The New World, Vol. 1: Before 1775*. New York: Time-Life Books, 1963.

Reische, Diana. *Founding the American Colonies*. New York: Franklin Watts, 1989.

Roop, Connie and Peter Roop. *Pilgrim Voices: Our First Year in the New World*. New York: Walker and Company, 1995.

Scott, John Anthony. *Settlers on the Eastern Shore: The British Colonies in North America, 1607–1750*. New York: Facts on File, 1991.

Sherrow, Victoria. *Pennsylvania*. San Diego: Lucent Books, 2002.

Smith, Carter, ed. *The Explorers and Settlers*. Brookfield, Conn.: The Millbrook Press, 1991.

Streissguth, Thomas. *New Jersey*. San Diego: Lucent Books, 2002.

Webb, Robert N. *The Colony of Rhode Island*. New York: Franklin Watts, 1972.

Ziner, Feenie. *Squanto*. Hamden, Conn.: Linnet Books, 1988.

FOR MORE INFORMATION

Pilgrims and Plymouth Colony
pilgrims.net/plymouth/history

Massachusetts Bay Colony
www.usahistory.info/
New-England/Massachusetts

Rhode Island
www.rogerwilliams.org/biography

Connecticut
www.colonialwarsct.org/1636

New Netherland
www.newnetherland.org

New Sweden
www.colonialswedes.org/History/History

Pennsylvania
www.legis.state.pa.us/WU01/VC/visitor_info/
pa_history/II

INDEX

BIOGRAPHIES

AUTHOR

Sheila Nelson has always been fascinated with history and the lives of historical figures. She enjoys studying history and learning more about the events and people that have shaped our world. Sheila has written several books on history and other subjects. Recently, she completed a master's degree and now lives in Rochester, New York, with her husband and their baby daughter.

SERIES CONSULTANT

Dr. Jack N. Rakove is a professor of history and American studies at Stanford University, where he is director of American studies. The winner of the 1997 Pulitzer Prize in history, Dr. Rakove is the author of *The Unfinished Election of 2000, Constitutional Culture and Democratic Rule,* and *James Madison and the Creation of the American Republic.* He is also the president of the Society for the History of the Early American Republic.

PICTURE CREDITS

Connecticut Historical Society: p. 54
Corel: pp. 24–25
Dover: p. 30
The Freedom Trail: p. 11
Library of Congress: pp. 29, 81
Photos.com: pp. 60–61, 84–85, 86–87